First edition 2025

ISBN 978-1-7779609-4-0

This book was typeset in Cambria.
The illustrations were created via freehand sketch,
then digitally tweaked by yours truly.

The New Roommate Must GO!

An innocent family addition
tips the household balance,
revealing a fluffy,
purrfect companion.

Written & illustrated by
Heather Rae Beauchesne

Dedicated to Bri, Izzy, Ariel, Norie, Aidan & Rocky

For the first few weeks,
our new roommate was
so sweet, so meek, and
we all adored her.

Shorty after,
there was a change...

My bed, once my oasis
of bone-peppered dreams,
was now her throne.

Dinner scraps were no longer mine for the picking.

My body
became one of many
trampolines in her magical
gymnasium - once referred
to as 'the living room'.

Our nights, previously filled with tranquility and slumber, were transformed into night shifts requiring her watch.

Her guard post: my pillow.
Her seat: my head.

Our furniture, the rug, the other roommates' legs, ... my tail, were deemed appropriate scratching posts.

... But lately,

when she is
finished with her
own meal, she leaves
the clean-up to me.

When a cool day calls
for a sun-soaked nap,
she snuggles in
beside me.

She has become a promising student of olfaction. My most esteemed sniffing spots she inspects alongside me.

Sniff-Sniff.
mmm, oh, that's good.

Olfaction:
the action
or capacity
of smelling;
the sense
of smell.

And when the other
roommates are away,
and I am lonely,
she rubs up
against me with
sandpaper kisses
and soothing purrs.

After many sunny afternoons of deep reflection, bone gnawing, and thorough consideration of the new and improved household balance, the new roommate may stay.

About the Author

Heather Rae Beauchesne is a studio artist,
author-illustrator, gallery curator,
physical therapist, an advocate for
community arts, culture, and health & wellbeing,
and a fan of furry roommates.

The New Roommate Must Go! is the
sequel to Beauchesne's first children's book,
My Roommate is the Worst!

It's time
to build
your own
story.

.... get ready!

brain storm

Make a list of:

- cool things you have done: _____
_____
_____
_____

- stuff you seem to talk
  about ... a lot: _____
_____
_____
_____

- stuff you like to read
  or have read to you: _____
_____
_____
_____

- things you dream of: _____
  _____
  _____
  _____

- stuff you know a lot about: _____
  _____
  _____
  _____

- an experience that is
  uniquely yours: _____
  _____
  _____
  _____

Circle one or two items on your list that really pop-out.
Now we have a 'basic idea' of what we like, know a lot about,
and most importantly would like to tell others about.

create the parts

P.S. this is a rough sketch of the story. Don't spend too much time thinking about this; our best ideas are the first ones! It will all come together as you work through it :)

What is the main message of your story? What experience do you want to share? What lesson do you wish to teach?

(A.K.A. the title of your book)

The Big idea:
_____
_____
_____
_____

Describe your story's character(s), setting, and problem/goal/experience that will be the focus of your story.

Character(s):
_____
_____
_____

Setting:
_____
_____
_____

Problem/goal/experience:
_____
_____
_____

Remember, anything goes, this is your world, your story.

The beginning:
create a few sentences,
per scene, that introduce
your readers to the
character(s) and the
problem/goal/experience.
(The setting will be captured in
your sketches for those scenes.)

Scene 1: _____
_____
_____
_____

Scene 2: _____
_____
_____
_____

The middle:
In 2 scenes,
outline how the character's
problem/goal comes
to a turning point or a
key event/experience
takes place.

*Don't forget to include
the funny parts!*

Scene 1: _____
_____
_____
_____

Scene 2: _____
_____
_____
_____

The end:
In 2 scenes,
describe how the problem
is solved, or the goal
has been achieved.
Has the main character
learned something?
What is the final scene
and line of the book
(the closure or message)?

Scene 1: _____
_____
_____
_____

Scene 2: _____
_____
_____
_____

sketch practice

cool colourz

Have fun with making silly characters and scenes here.
This will help you find your illustration style!

Are you ready to put it all together? ↘

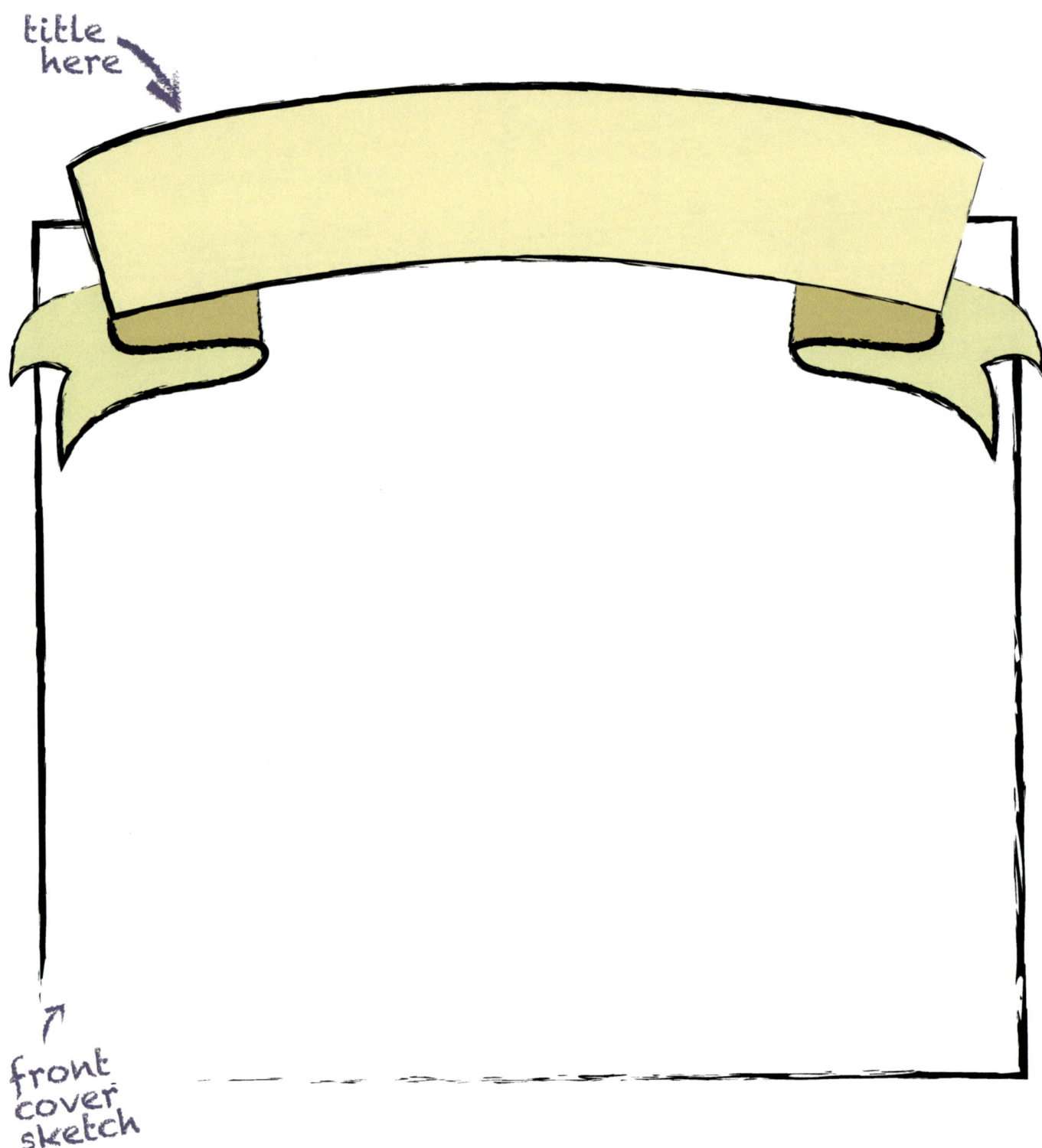

title here

front cover sketch

written by: _____

illustrated by: _____

dedicated to: _____

copyright date: _____

the beginning

the middle

the end

About the Author

tell us all about you

sketch or
photo of
you here

Manufactured by Amazon.ca
Bolton, ON

51171106R00036